EssaySnark's Strategies for the
2014-'15 MBA Application for
TUCK SCHOOL OF BUSINESS

EssaySnark's Strategies for the 2014-'15 MBA Application for TUCK SCHOOL OF BUSINESS

by EssaySnark®

Snarkolicious Press

First edition published October 27, 2011
2014 version 4.0 published May 24, 2014

Snarkolicious Press
P. O. Box 50021
Palo Alto, CA 94303

www.snarkoliciouspress.com

978 1 938098 22 2

© 2011-2014 by EssaySnark®

Cover image © Eric Isselée, used under license from Fotolia.com

All rights reserved. No part of this book may be reproduced or transmitted in any form or by any means, electronic or mechanical, including photocopying, recording, transcribing, or by an information storage system, without permission from the publisher. Essay questions copyright Dartmouth Tuck.

This publication is provided "as is", without warranty of any kind, either express or implied. The author and Snarkolicious Press assume no liability for errors or omissions in this publication or other documents which are referenced or linked to this publication. While we certainly hope that you will be successful in your quest for admission to an MBA program, we cannot offer any promises that you will be, whether or not you adopt the advice provided herein. In no event shall Snarkolicious Press or its authors, principals, subsidiaries, partners, or owners be liable for any special, incidental, indirect or consequential damages of any kind, or any damages whatsoever, arising out of or in conjunction with the use or performance of this information. Applicants to any graduate program or university should verify the school's policies, application requirements, processes, procedures, and other criteria. This publication could include technical or other inaccuracies or typographical errors. Changes are periodically added to the information herein; these changes will be incorporated into new editions of this publication. Thus, different versions or formats of this publication may include different information.

Look for other *SnarkStrategies Guides* (digital and paperback) at your favorite bookseller or on the EssaySnark blahg at http://essaysnark.com.

Follow EssaySnark on Twitter!

"Not saying they're right. Not saying they're wrong. But will say they are snarky! re: @essaysnark Good dose of humor and kick in the pants."

*@TuckAdmissions tweet about
EssaySnark's Tuck essay advice, 9/22/11*

We Love Tuck

EssaySnark is enamored of Tuck. If we could go get our MBA over again, we'd want to go to Dartmouth. Tuck is one of our absolute favoritist schools. This *SnarkStrategies Guide* explains why.

If you don't want to read the whole thing to find out, the essence of it is, Tuck is a) very small; b) very intimate; and c) very beautiful. It's also a darn good education. Tuck is a place where lasting relationships are formed. It's a place where you can get to know your professors – and no, that absolutely does not happen at many of the big schools in the big cities. Tuck is a place where you have nothing else to do but what you came to bschool for: to learn.

Mother Nature is the biggest distraction at Tuck – and while she can be a mighty temptress, luring you out into the mountains with snowshoes or snowboard or a pair of hiking boots in fall or late spring, she also does her part to make you huddle together with your sectionmates and your case studies by dumping so much snow that it shuts the place down on a regular basis. (How much snow? We'll tell you on page 2.)

The other thing you should be aware of is some negative media that Dartmouth College received in spring 2014, which we do not believe impacts the Tuck students but you need to know about it:

Philip Hanlon, president of Dartmouth College since 2012, has gone out on a campaign to change the partying/hazing/sexual abuse culture that's been predominant at this school for generations. Just so you know, the Jim Belushi movie *Animal House* from the 1970s about a partying fraternity at a college campus was loosely based on Dartmouth. You're probably too young to know about *Animal House* or Jim Belushi, so ask your parents. ☺

You can Google "Dartmouth hazing" and you'll get a flurry of hits dating back for many years. Here's a couple links in case you're interested:

- *Rolling Stone* piece from 2012 on Dartmouth's frat culture: http://rol.st/1I5fjEZ
- Text of President Hanlon's speech from April 2014: http://wapo.st/1j70pIF
- *Washington Post* coverage: http://wapo.st/1m8WEaT

Just like at other schools, MBA students at Dartmouth tend to be rather isolated from the undergrad population – Tuckies definitely form bonds with other Tuckies, first and foremost – so this may be a non-issue for you. But you should know about it, particularly if you have a news junkie gramma who hears you're going to go to Dartmouth and freaks out about it. You need to know the facts.

What you must do to have a chance at Tuck

Now, applying to any top MBA program is a big undertaking. You have to put in your time, and the essays are a bear. This is true everywhere. It's perhaps *more true* at Tuck. Before we get too far with this *SnarkStrategies Guide*, we need to advise you that you must make a bigger commitment to the application process at Tuck than at almost any other school.

In fact, this is so important we're going to throw out a set-in-stone rule for you to ponder, right here on the first page:

Snarky Strategy #1

If you're serious about Tuck,
you must visit the school before you apply.

Tuck actually tells you this. They want you to come visit. They invite you – all of you – to interview on campus. They want you to know what their school, and Hanover, is like.

We go into all the details of why and how later, but we wanted to lay it out upfront: EssaySnark *strongly* feels that you *must* visit campus *before* you submit your application.

OK great. Now let's finish the conversation around why we love Tuck so much, so that you can get excited about the prospect of that visit.

One reason is that Tuck has earned our fondness. In our many years working with stressed-out Brave Supplicants, EssaySnark appreciates the openness and transparency that the Tuck admissions department tries to impart upon their processes. Their website gives straightforward, practical answers to important questions that can have a real effect on outcomes. There are plenty of other schools with applicant-friendly admissions offices – Darden, Ross, and Booth all come immediately to mind in this category. This is not meant as an exhaustive list. And, you wouldn't want to pick a bschool just because their admissions people are nice. But it sure doesn't hurt. The MBA admissions process is onerous enough without it seeming like the school is trying to trick you, based on confusing policies and secretive procedures.

Another reason why we love Tuck? Because nobody's heard of it. Ask a random person on the street what the best business school is, and they'll probably say Harvard or Stanford or Wharton. Even though *The Economist* picked Tuck the best school in the world in 2011 – they dropped back to #2 in 2012 – most people wouldn't name them. They might not even know that Dartmouth has a business school.

That sounds crazy. EssaySnark likes Tuck because nobody's heard of them? What logic is that?

People who know bschools – the recruiters at the best firms, business leaders with a clue – the class of folk who EssaySnark likes to call the connoisseurs *of the business education*, of which EssaySnark likes to consider ourself one too – call us *EssaySnob*, perhaps – these people understand what Tuck is. The people who end up at Tuck, the students and professors who call it home, they know its value. They've done their research and sought it out. And that makes for a very powerful environment. Everyone who's at Tuck really wants to be there; you don't just stumble into the place. A school like Chicago, or UCLA, it's possible to end up at one of these places by convenience. You were living in the area and you decided to go to bschool, and whaddya know, they let you in. Not so with Tuck. You have to *know* about it. You have to make an effort. There's something about this reality of Tuck that we just appreciate.

Just because EssaySnark – or your best friend's dad, or *The Economist* – says they love Tuck doesn't automatically mean that you should, too. A Tuck application is *a lot* of work – what other school asks you to trek all the way to New Hampshire to have a go at things? If you're serious about Tuck you'll need to prove it to them.

Tuck is like the belle of the ball, lots of suitors seek her hand but she will only dance with those who show themselves sincere.

We're stuck on Tuck. Of course, if you find yourself stuck on your Tuck essays, email your question to gethelpnow@essaysnark.com and we'll see what we can do to help out.

We also have a separate *Tuck Scholarship Essay QuickSnark Guide* available for instant-access purchase on essaysnark.com.

Good luck with Tuck!

Table of Contents

Some Quick Tuck Facts..1
Important Considerations: How Much Snow?..2
For Whom Is Tuck Looking – and Who Should Consider Tuck?.....................3
    What does Tuck need to see in your profile?..5
Do I Really Have to Visit?..8
Your GMAT Score and Tuck..11
Tuck's Application Rounds and Policies..14
    What is Early Action?..15
    When should you apply?...16
    The 7 steps to a Tuck application 17
    Multi-school strategies..18
Planning Your Tuck Essays...19
    What's the right balance of topics?...19
Essay 1: Career Goals..21
Essay 2: Leadership...31
    "Collaborative" Leadership?...31
    How to choose a story for Tuck essay 2..32
    What did you learn?..35
Letters of Recommendation..39
International Experience...40
Optional Essay..41
The Tuck Interview...43
What to Do Next...45

Some Quick Tuck Facts

To get this party started, here's a few quick facts:

> **Tuck typically admits 450 to 500 students -- 17% to 20% of the applicant pool -- with about 270 enrolling.**

And another:

> **The Class of 2014 had a mean/median salary of $115k per year (wow).**

And:

> **There was a 42-year-old graduating in that same class.**

It's pretty rare for someone of such advanced years to be admitted to ANY top bschool, but it does happen, so we wanted to toss out that little nugget.

One more datapoint:

> **The mean GMAT score has hovered between 717 and 718 for several years now.**

In case you're not aware, that's pretty darn high. That doesn't mean you're a goner if your GMAT score is on the low end, but most successful applications to this school come in with > 700 scores. We cover all of this in detail starting on page 11.

Regardless of your age or GMAT score, if you want to be one of those lucky Tuck graduates in a few years, then you have some work to do to make it in -- and you came to the right place by picking up this guide!

But before you seriously consider an application to Tuck, you must seriously consider one very important issue: Do you know how much it snows there?

Important Considerations: How Much Snow?

If you've lived in the mountains before, great! You know what to expect. If not – if you've never lived in a place that has real seasons – then here's some facts to make it real:

- The first snow comes around the beginning of November – before it's even officially winter!

- The last snow finally melts in May – well after the calendar has turned to spring!

- The total snowfall is at least 60 inches; it was a lot more than that in the winter of 2013-'14, when the entire East Coast was pummeled with storm after storm. February 2014 alone saw close to 30 inches of snow in Hanover, with almost 10 inches on one single day.

The other big factor to consider is a very small one: the town of Hanover, New Hampshire, where Dartmouth is located, is *tiny*. Under 12,000 people tiny. Many Brave Supplicants seek out a bschool that's in a city, so they can ~~party~~ explore the culture of a major metropolis for two years. Pretty much everyone who applies to Columbia cites its location in the "finance capital of the world" as a main reason they want to go there; in fact, Columbia even made that part of an essay question in 2013. Tuck is basically the exact opposite of New York. It's a sleepy little place, in the quintessential college town – not much going on in Hanover besides Dartmouth – where people go to learn stuff. There's an awful lot of reasons for people to go to New York City, and "learn stuff" is likely not the top of the list for the majority of them.

While Tuck is remote, it's still accessible. Day trips to Boston (2 hours) and New York (5 hours) are possible; Montreal is less than 4 hours away. The Vermonter Amtrak train runs from White River Junction and takes you to Manhattan or DC, though that's a more involved affair time-wise. Smaller airports are in Manchester, New Hampshire, and in Burlington, Vermont, or you can fly into Boston. Most Tuckies came from big cities before choosing New Hampshire for their two years of graduate school, and most will move away from Hanover again when their time at Tuck is over. Thus, it is a place where ideas are imported along with each entering class, and it remains ever new.

So, the culture of Tuck is as much created by these surroundings and the reality of its environment as it is by the actual business school academics and the people of Dartmouth. Factor in the general appreciation for the outdoors and a concern for preserving natural resources that are common among Tuckies and you have a very unique and vibrant atmosphere for business education at Dartmouth.

For Whom Is Tuck Looking – and Who Should Consider Tuck?

Like other top schools, Tuck is interested in diversity in their student body across every spectrum imaginable – race, ethnicity, gender, sexual orientation, socioeconomic background, career history, career interest. Of all the types of potential MBA student out there, who should specifically consider applying to Tuck?

In other words, which types of candidates might have an easier time of admission – and/or which types would be especially suited for Tuck?

- **International students.** Many overseas candidates seem to prefer schools in larger cities. Even Duke is in a bigger city than Tuck. Accordingly, Tuck gets proportionally fewer applications from international candidates than other top-ranked schools. If you're coming from a foreign land, and you know why you want to go to Tuck, they may be especially receptive to an application from you.

- **International experience.** No matter what your nationality, if you have work experience outside your home country, you're going to be more appealing to the Tuck admissions team (see page 40 for a separate in-app question that they ask about this).

- **Women.** Perhaps just due to the fact that Tuck is a bit of a sleeper brand, there are also fewer females applying. Tuck has one of the lower ratios of women to men than other top schools. They're always on the lookout for strong female candidates. If that's you, and you can make a case why you want to go to Tuck, you may have a relatively easy time in securing an offer from them.

- **African-Americans, Hispanics, and other U.S. minorities.** For possibly the same reasons – the fact that the "Tuck" name is not as well known as "Harvard" despite the fact that it's top-ranked by many major publications – Tuck doesn't get as many applications from underrepresented classes than many schools. Tuck is a member of The Consortium, and they are working hard to attract more diverse candidates with special outreach programs and targeted efforts such as Diversity Days, etc. If you're a minority candidate with a track record of success, and you can see yourself in Hanover, you should most definitely give it a shot.

- **Snowboarders.** Well.... maybe it's not about snowboarders getting into Tuck in greater numbers, but it's certainly true that snowboarders will have a lot to like during their time there. Skiers too. And all other lovers of the Great Outdoors (that's not gonna be enough to get you in but it makes Dartmouth a sure draw for many folks).

- **Hockey players.** Ditto the above comment, with the added advantage that Tuck is always looking for ways to strengthen its hockey team.

- **Private equity guys.** Tuck is known as a general management program – which means it's perfect for anyone who wants to go into consulting and can be an ideal foundation for a wide range of other career paths. What is less commonly known is that Tuck is held in high regard by the private equity community. There are strong ties to Tuck in many areas of finance, yet if you're specifically interested in PE, you would be well advised to keep Tuck on your short list.

- **Military guys (and women!).** Partly due to Tuck's preference for older candidates with more work experience, and partly due to its appreciation for what the military imparts in terms of leadership and maturity, and even more so due to the broad and strong general management education you can get there, Tuck is an ideal choice for many candidates who are separating from the military. If you're currently on active duty or you recently completed your service, the Tuck admissions committee will pay close attention to your application. And if you're a woman separating from the service, you'd likely be in high demand at Tuck (or at any top program!).

- **Marrieds/with childrens.** A higher percentage of Tuckies are married than at most schools; Duke is another school where it's also common to be married. Tuck can be a great choice for anyone with a family, provided your spouse doesn't need to get a job in the town where you're going to bschool (not a lot of industry in Hanover). If you're single, keep in mind that while Tuckies still know how to have a good time, Tuck is much less a party school than many other top MBA programs. Happy hour is a big part of the culture at any of the big-city bschools. This is slightly less true at Tuck, partly due to the environment – not quite as many opportunities to go out on the town, because there's not so much of a town – and also because Tuck students are a bit older, so perhaps they have more of their partying days behind them. And, as just noted, more of them are married. (Note that *Dartmouth College* has a reputation as an intense party school among the undergrads; we'll talk about this a bit later.) The Tuck community does a great job of embracing students' spouses and providing plenty of opportunities for them to network and socialize, with support and activities for kids, too. Tuck has even has had Tuck Partners contributing to their student blog, which gives a nice perspective. This type of warm and welcoming environment for significant others is not as prevalent at some of Tuck's peer programs around the country – though to be real, if your spouse needs to find a job in the locale where you move for bschool, it's going to be pretty difficult for that in Hanover, New Hampshire. Stay-at-home parents may find Tuck to be bschool nirvana; working spouses may feel more challenged by Tuck as your choice.

What does Tuck need to see in your profile?

To have a real shot at Tuck, the adcom will want to see certain characteristics or traits come through loud and clear in the different aspects of your application. Specifically, they want to see evidence that you are:

1. **Experienced.** You need to have *done something* before you try for Tuck. Five years of work experience is average; they'll consider you with somewhat less, but not too much less. If you have three or fewer years of career history, and you're bound and determined to go to bschool next year, you may want to try for a different school than Tuck. And, Tuck wants to see more than just quantity; it's not enough to have accumulated five years in the workforce, you need to show evidence of accomplishment. A couple promotions or a significant jump to a new level in responsibility will be critically important to demonstrate that you're a hard worker who's got drive and determination.

2. **Committed.** Probably the number one thing that Tuck looks for in your application is evidence that you understand what they're about and are choosing them first. Tuck is never a "safety school"; you won't have a chance here if you don't do your homework in advance and appropriately communicate why you're excited about what they offer[1]. If there's any hint of ambivalence – if it appears at all that you're going through the motions, that you're not 100% committed to Tuck, or most importantly, that you don't understand what they're about – then it's quite easy for the admissions folks to take a pass on you.

3. **Accomplished.** While the GMAT score is certainly not the most important factor in admissions at Tuck, students there do have a high average, bumping up to 718 for the Class of 2015 (the most recent data available at the time of this writing). In a typical year, 40% of Tuck students have a GMAT score from 720 to 760; another 10% are even higher than that. (We'll talk more about GMAT in a bit.) Average GPA is 3.5, which is towards the higher end of the range of other top schools (Harvard = 3.6, Cornell = 3.3). Beyond the mere numbers, Tuck will also want to see evidence of how you've contributed to the world around you, how you've had an impact on the job – gee, didn't we sort of cover some of this stuff already, when we talked about experience? Yes, it all wraps together. They will seek to be impressed in the whole package.

4. **Humble.** Given the small size of the program, and the essentially 24/7 environment, where you'll be living and studying with the same people in close proximity for an intense and extended period of time, Tuck needs to make sure that the students they accept are cool. A jerk-o on campus can ruin things for everyone. Sometimes, candidates come across a little strong in their essays. In an effort to sound

---

[1] Note: EssaySnark is not gonna directly come out and state this. We're not gonna tell you the secret sauce. That's for you to create on your own, through your individual concoction of essays!

impressive, they come off sounding arrogant. (Sometimes, they really are arrogant. Yes, we know that's not you, dear Brave Supplicant!!) This is one key value that a (good!) admissions consultant can add to your process: they can read your essays and let you know if you're coming on too strong, or if you could be inadvertently tripping the *No Thanks!* switch in the reader's mind. Tuck won't be touching you with the metaphorical ten-foot pole if you've got yucky oozing out anywhere. If you know yourself to be brash or headstrong, there's other schools that aren't quite as sensitive to such qualities. If you're simply confident, just make sure it doesn't come on too strong in your presentation. Confident is good; cocky, not so much.

So those are the keys.... and you also cannot already have an MBA (you can possibly have a PGP from India but you need to explain why you also need an MBA) – but wait. Let's back up.

We said "committed." How the heck do you show that? What does "ambivalent" or "not 100% committed" look like?

Well, if you do a save-as on your essays for Berkeley, for example, and you forget to change "Haas" to "Tuck" before submitting them... that's not going to go over so well in Hanover. Even worse if it was a Harvard essay that you repurposed. Or, if you just have lackluster essays that don't ooze with sincerity and give solid reasons for wanting to come – like, with direct references to the stuff that Tuck offers, the unique elements and aspects of their program – they're gonna wonder if you're serious.

Or, if you couldn't be bothered to visit campus and interview prior to applying. We covered this last point before, and we'll do more on it later... keep reading.

Work experience appears first in the above list, because the door to admissions won't even be open to you unless you've got the solid foundation of a career established. That door to admissions will slam firmly shut again, however, if you fail to convince the admissions committee that you're serious about wanting to go there. Or if you sound like an arrogant ass...

Many bschools are focused on culture and fit these days. Besides Tuck, others that put a premium on this include NYU, Duke, Ross, Darden, and Berkeley-Haas.

In fact, Haas has some other things in common with Tuck as well. Let's do a comparison so that you can see how two specific similar but different schools stack up.

A tale of two bschools

In terms of class profile, Tuck is almost a mirror image of the Haas School, minus Berkeley's Birkenstocks and patchouli. There are obviously big differences in the macro environments of these two schools: The State of New Hampshire's population of 1.3 million is largely Republican-leaning, with a strong Libertarian orientation, while Berkeley and the San

Francisco Bay Area's 7.15 million people are on the opposite side of the political spectrum (Democrat/liberal with a good share of Libertarian too). Berkeley is a much busier, bustling place. Haas has a business undergraduate program, too, so there are many more students around their business school; plus, the entire UC-Berkeley university has a population of about 35,000 students, compared to Dartmouth's total of just 6,000. So these are very different places.

But if you take the microcosms of the bschools themselves, here's how the two business schools break down along the standard admissions dimensions:

	Tuck	Haas
Typical Class Size	270	240
Average GMAT Score	718	715
Median GMAT Score	720	720
80% Range of GMAT Scores	680-760	680-760
Number of Applications	2,600	3,400
Acceptance Rate	about 20%	about 14%
Yield	55%	56%
Number of Letters in School Name	4	4
Annual Snowfall	at least 60"	0"

Admissions data are for the Class of 2015

Besides these similar datapoints, both of these schools are notable based on how distinctive their cultures are – at least in terms of values and student attitudes about what they want their bschool experience to be like. None of this is to suggest that Berkeley and Haas offer identical educations. Both are very good MBA programs, considered Top 10 by most anyone's standard. Yet each has its own specialties and slants.

Berkeley has the legacy of its gazillion Nobel laureates in economics on faculty past and present. Dartmouth is stronger in finance overall, partly due to its (relative) proximity to Wall Street. Berkeley is also considered a more regional program, because a huge number of its graduates stay in the West when they finish, which then means that future job opportunities are often concentrated in the region due to even stronger corporate connections in the same area from those alumni. The Cal brand name has less clout around the world than Dartmouth does. Tuck is a much older MBA program and so it has a larger alumni network, but not by a whole lot. Students at both schools tend to have a heightened awareness of and commitment to social causes and the environment than you'll find at other bschools. Some students may feel equally at home at both campuses, though certainly not all would, given the differences in environment and the respective surrounding regions.

This comparison is offered so that you can get insight into the various dimensions of an MBA program, and start to think about the potential value and benefits available from attending one type of school versus another. None of this is meant to say that Tuck is better than Berkeley (or vice versa) but instead, this brief discussion should hopefully help you learn more about the various criteria by which you can judge a specific program, to better evaluate how it fits with your own interests and needs in graduate business education.

And now, back to our regularly scheduled program of advising you on your best-bet strategy for how to make a strong showing in an application to Dartmouth's Tuck School of Business.

Let's start with the first part, the one where EssaySnark says yes, it's true, you do have to make an investment. You gotta get on a plane and go for a ride.

Do I Really Have to Visit?

"I'm so busy... and it's expensive."

Riiiiiight.

We already gave you this first rule of the road back in the preamble to this *Guide*, but we'll repeat it here in case you missed it the first time:

Snarky Strategy #1

If you're serious about Tuck,
you must visit the school before you apply.

On the Tuck website, and in their messaging to candidates, they lay out the facts that getting an MBA is a significant investment of time and money – a true statement that is often overlooked in the excitement of applying to schools. And they tell you point blank that you should do your research, *including a visit to campus*, so that you can better learn what they're about, IN ADVANCE OF APPLYING. They don't just assume that you'll love it once you get there.

In fact, because of how different the place is – up in the mountains and such – the Tuck administration wants to avoid any shock to the system that may otherwise occur if a Brave Supplicant applies to their great school, and is admitted, sight unseen. They're doing all they can to weed out the tire-kickers and the not-quite-committed types *before* those people apply. Plenty of people do that at other schools each year – they apply, and are accepted, and do not set one foot on campus until the admit weekend (sometimes not even until they matriculate!). Tuck doesn't want that to happen there.

Because so many people use bschool rankings systems as their only criteria in determining which schools to apply to, Tuck has an open interview policy, and a direct *please-come-interview-in-advance* invitation to all applicants. To quote the admissions people directly, "Everybody has an opportunity to interview, but not everybody *takes advantage of it.*" (emphasis ours) They end up interviewing about a third of all candidates – and they've done some analysis on who ends up getting accepted, and the numbers turn out to favor the ones who came for the open interview.

EssaySnark also believes that this liberal interview policy is designed at least in part as means for admissions to winnow the field. Unlike many schools, Tuck does *not* seem to want everyone and her brother to apply. Yes, they want a large pool of qualified and committed candidates to select from, but the "qualified" and "committed" parts are much more important than the "large pool" part is at Tuck. Most of all, they don't want to accept someone who is clueless about what Tuck is like.

This is why Tuck offers candidate-initiated interviews, to anyone who is interested, conducted on campus throughout the admissions season. And this is why they strongly encourage everyone to come interview before submitting an application. This visit is not required, but it's really strongly you-should-do-it-if-you're-serious recommended. Yes, they know that it's inconvenient, and they know that it can be expensive. And yet they still want you to do it – even if (or perhaps ESPECIALLY if) you live in Europe or Asia or some other faraway place. Their online application even asks you to explain why you did not do the pre-application interview if you don't have one scheduled at the time you submit. That's pretty direct.

Bschool is expensive. Tuck is unique, both in geography and in the bschool experience that they offer. Those two factors could add up to a serious case of buyer's remorse if you weren't paying attention before applying.

Now, the fact is, it's highly unlikely that someone could demonstrate significant knowledge of and enthusiasm for this school in his essays *without* having the experience of being on campus and meeting the people. It's certainly possible, but unlikely. This is a case where attending an info session in your city is a good first step, but you should not bank on that as being enough exposure to the school. If you want to make a compelling case for your candidacy, ya gotta get to Hanover.

This is not to say that Tuck won't even consider you if you don't make it up to campus before applying. If they like you enough, and you didn't interview in advance, then they may invite you to come interview as part of their evaluation. EssaySnark suspects that most everyone accepted at Tuck is interviewed first (though it's not officially mandatory to be interviewed before accepted). Yes, they absolutely will make accommodations for interviewing in very special circumstances, such as active-duty military on deployment; phone interviews with an admissions team member are common in such cases.

But since you're likely to get interviewed before you'd be accepted anyway, why not make the effort in advance, when it can benefit *you* the most, and head up to New Hampshire early, while you're still crafting your application strategy and figuring out what to talk about in those essays?

Here are the benefits of visiting Tuck before you apply:

- **Research.** Meeting the admissions people, sitting in on a class, and walking through the halls of the school are the absolute best ways to learn about what it can offer. You can get a lot more questions answered in a day being immersed with the students – and you can understand significantly better what a Tuck MBA is all about – by experiencing it firsthand, than you can from reading a website.

- **Interaction.** Depending on when you go, of course, you can potentially meet a lot more Tuckies when you're on campus than you ever could at an info session in your hometown. (Be sure to check the calendar to confirm that classes are in session and students will be around at the time that you want to come visit.) How better to find out if you feel at home with the people you're theoretically going to spend a very intimate two years with, than to go meet them on their turf?

- **Appreciation.** New Hampshire is gorgeous, and Tuck is special. Maybe you know that. Seeing it for yourself may give you that much more motivation to want to make it your home for two years. And, the culture of a school can best be understood when you're on campus. This is true at any bschool, it's pointedly true at Tuck.

- **Interview.** Last but not least, traveling to campus lets you interview directly with the admissions team. The staff at Tuck are exceptionally friendly. You'll likely be interviewed by an equally friendly second-year student. You can expect the interview to be low-key and low-stress. It's still a critical part of your application – don't underestimate its importance just because it's open to anyone and they're nice. You'll want to prepare carefully. However you don't have to get too worked up about it. It's typically reported to be an enjoyable experience. Additional tips and insights for the Tuck interview are provided later in this *Guide;* you may also want to also pick up our separate interviewing guide for an in-depth explanation of the best ways to prepare for such an important opportunity.

All of these benefits of the Tuck visit can be leveraged in your essays. What better way to demonstrate your enthusiasm for the school than being able to talk about the people you met and the experiences you had when you were on campus? That can go a long way to showing the adcom why you want an MBA – and why you want to go to Tuck to earn it.

Your GMAT Score and Tuck

Tuck is a tiny school with a massively high average GMAT score.

That's sort of not great for someone with only a mediocre GMAT.

- They have around 250 to 280 students per class.
  Recent years have had larger classes.

- The average test score of that very small population is very high:
  718 for the Class of 2015.

What that means is, pretty much everyone in the class did really well on the test. And what *that* means is, pretty much everyone they accept did really well. (Obviously a school with a larger student population can have more students with lower scores, which would be balanced out, on average, by the higher-scoring students.) At Dartmouth, pretty much all the MBA students have impressive GMATs.

To be a competitive candidate at Tuck (or any school), it's best to present a profile that matches most of the parameters of their accepted students. They have published an overall range for students in the Class of 2015 of GMAT scores of 530 to 780 – but don't think you're going to be the one skating in with the < 600 GMAT. Every school admits one or two outliers each year. Don't count on that being you.

Based on EssaySnark's imprecise analysis of the data available, we believe that the majority of Tuck students score well over 700 on the GMAT.

The best part about how Tuck treats your GMAT?

They let you mix-and-match your scores!

There is no other top bschool on the planet – at least, none that we've heard of – that will do this. Tuck lets you report your best quant score, and best verbal score, *even if they're from different test dates!* Truly unheard of, and truly applicant-friendly. This is one of the many admissions policies in place that makes EssaySnark love Tuck[2]. They also will consider a GRE score – which all top schools do – but they'll look at it in conjunction with a GMAT score too. You can submit up to two of each and they'll check out the entire history to see what they might see.

Regardless of this flexibility, your overall GMAT (or GRE) score still matters.

---

2 http://essaysnark.com/2010/10/adcoms-that-we-trust.html

Let's break it down.

- If your GMAT score is less than 670, it's not impossible to get an offer at Tuck, but you're not making it easy on yourself.

- If your score is 660? Sure, go for it. Submit your application. You're within range of reality – as long as you're not coming from an oversubscribed population like Indian engineers. If you are, then go for > 700 if you're serious abut this place.

- If your score is lower than 660, we don't have high hopes. You should take a hard look at your candidacy. You need to either make sure you're presenting proof of quant skills elsewhere in the application, or consider taking a class to help shore up your strengths (and then maybe even re-test the GMAT in order to present a happier score to the adcom).

The bottom line is, yes, you can get into Tuck with a lower GMAT score – even a score way below 650 – but, just like at any other school, it's much easier if your total score is above 700. If you're at least at the 660 to 680 range, EssaySnark is reasonably comfortable. Maybe not overly confident, but not massively concerned – provided you do your homework and the rest of your application lines up.

But just like with other schools, if your GMAT is on the low side (<660), and your academic history doesn't show that you've excelled in quant-based classes before – and especially if you've never worked with numbers much – you should think of taking a class to bolster your profile. We won't hold out much hope for you otherwise. Sorry but that's just how the puzzle pieces fit together.

Since we're on the subject of the GMAT, let's toss out an important tip to keep in mind at Tuck:

A Snarky Caveat

Tuck will accept the GRE, but they prefer the GMAT.

They used to state this preference on their website. They don't have it in black and white anymore which means if you have a GRE score, feel confident in using that – but our bet is the only reason it's not on the website is so that they don't discourage anyone. If you have a choice in which test to take, please choose the GMAT. If you already have a GRE – and it's decent – then move forward with that.

Other schools, we suspect, also prefer the GMAT, but they're not advertising that fact, since the whole point of accepting both tests is to increase the applicant pool. The latest trend in bschool policies has been openness and invitation. The schools are all in a race to get more applications than the other school. They'd hate to shoot themselves in the foot in that statistic just because someone decides not to apply with a GRE in hand.

But if you're applying for just the MBA – and you're truly serious about getting it from Tuck – you'd be better off submitting a GMAT score with your application. The GRE is just not held in as high regard as the GMAT; it is considered an easier test. Most bschools don't have a deep dataset on past candidates and accepted students who submitted the GRE test with their applications. Thus, the schools have little to go on and cannot use the GRE as a predictor for new candidate pools to the same degree as they can the GMAT.

One final point about GMAT scores:

A Snarky Caveat

Tuck must have RECEIVED
your official score report by the application deadline.

This is stated clearly in their FAQ but this policy is different from many other schools, so we're calling it out for you here. Other schools let you key in the unofficial score data when completing your app and then they'll marry up the official report later. Tuck needs you to submit the official data in the application.

This policy means that you can't put off your GMAT (re)test till the last minute. Tuck says it takes about six days for a school to receive the official score from the GMAC after you request it to be sent to the schools, but GMAC says that it can be *up to three weeks after a test* for the official results, including the AWA, to become available. (We don't know how long it takes for GREs.)

To be conservative, you should plan on taking the GMAT at least three weeks before the Tuck deadline that you're targeting.

Tuck's Application Rounds and Policies

Tuck has four application rounds. The first, called *Early Action*, might confuse someone who has done research on Columbia and knows about their Early Decision option – or Duke's Early Action. These three schools' application processes are not the same.

- Tuck's Early Action Round demonstrates this school's applicant-friendliness: **it is not binding**.
- Duke Early Action and Columbia Early Decision are binding.

We've got more details on Early Action below, including information on how it's different from Columbia and Duke. For now, you should just know that these application processes, like the schools that offer them, are very, very different[3].

OK, so Tuck has four rounds. Like with any other top MBA program, it's to your advantage to apply in the earliest round for which you are ready. If you have your act together for Early Action, great! Go for it! If you do not yet have all the pieces in place – then wait. The November Round is also a very viable application option, as is the January Round. A strong application will have a good chance at Tuck if submitted for any of those three deadlines.

However, EssaySnark always always always advises against applying in any school's last round. So, for Tuck, if you're looking at the April Round – you should strongly consider skipping it entirely and just wait through the summer in order to apply for the Early Action Round the following October. For a discussion of the reasons why, check out this blahg post:

http://essaysnark.com/2011/02/considering-applying-to-bschool-now.html

Even more confusing with Tuck and rounds is they have a different set of deadlines for Consortium applicants, *plus* they have other deadlines for applying for their scholarships. Be sure to study these dates so you understand them.

http://www.tuck.dartmouth.edu/admissions/important-dates

There is no Early Action option for Consortium candidates so even if you are an appropriate applicant through the Consortium, if you're really really serious about Tuck then you may as well go for their EA round.

The challenge for some people with pulling off an Tuck Early Action application is, of course, the in-advance interview. Many Brave Supplicants seem to only get their MBA application game on in September. And, huge numbers of you don't *really* start working on applications until late in September. At which point, it's basically impossible to get on campus for the tour and interview, at least, not before the app is actually due. Those October spots fill up fast.

---

3   Someone interested in and appropriate for Tuck might have a profile that would also be appealing to Columbia – but man oh man, these schools are so different. If you're interested in Tuck, are you *really* sure you're interested in Columbia? Might want to do some more research and validate your hypothesis on the best fit for you before proceeding.

You can still apply by the EA deadline and then interview after your app is in, but that's not ideal, because you then have less opportunity to talk in your essays about the really important school culture stuff that you learn from your visit.

If you got to this process late and it's like September, and you're considering whether to do an Early Action application without the interview, or alternatively the November Round (or even January Round) *with* the interview – generally, EssaySnark recommends deferring the application to the later round in order to apply with the interview, too. There may be some exceptions to this, and you'll need to weigh out all the options within the context of your overall MBA application strategy, but that's the way we'd be leaning if some Brave Supplicant asked us for advice on it.

What is Early Action?

Applying in the Early Action round can be a big benefit for many people – not nearly as much as it is for Columbia's Early Decision, but still, it can be an advantage at Tuck. You should study the Columbia website (and especially the *SnarkStrategies Guide for Columbia*) if you are interested in their Early Decision option, which is rolling, and binding, and thus a different animal entirely from what Tuck offers.

You can find a post about Early Decision on the EssaySnark blahg here:

http://essaysnark.com/2010/07/round-strategies-whats-this-early.html

Tuck's Early Action Round is designed to give you the quickest decision possible, and they offer it as an opportunity for those who are most enthusiastic and especially prepared. The application deadline (early October) and decision release date (mid-December) for Tuck Early Action both align with many other schools' Round 1. However, if Tuck accepts your Early Action application, then you'll need to pay a hefty $4,000 deposit in early January – and some schools won't have issued final Round 1 decisions by that time, and no schools will have offered their Welcome Weekend events yet. So you'd need to make your Tuck decision without as much of an extended opportunity of weighing out any other offers you may have received.

So, just like with any other schools' "early" process, you should be certain that Tuck is your #1 choice before applying. If, for example, you applied to Tuck Early Action and MIT or Haas Round 1, you would likely not hear back from the other school before you'd need to pay your Tuck deposit.

A further note about the binding "Early" options at Columbia and Duke: You could technically apply to both Tuck Early Action and to Columbia Early Decision or Duke Early Action – one or the other, not both – however if you are admitted to one of those other schools, you would need to immediately withdraw your application from Tuck. If Columbia is your #1 choice, then maybe that would be a no-brainer. But if you've gotten this far in this *SnarkStrategies Guide on Tuck*... are you really sure that you'd be able to walk away from the opportunity to go to Dartmouth? It totally depends on you and your goals, and it's a very personal decision, however you know how EssaySnark feels about Tuck... Sure, we love Columbia, too, but Tuck...

If Tuck is on your short list, then you may want to think twice about applying to any other school that has a binding "early" process.

Snarky Strategy #2

> It's fine to apply to other schools in their first rounds along with Tuck Early Action, but think carefully before applying to any other schools' binding Early Decision/Action rounds along with Tuck.

When should you apply?

Here are the guidelines for when you should apply to Tuck:

- If you are in love with Tuck and you have your application butt in gear, apply Early Action. This means that you need the essays, recommendations, AND INTERVIEW scheduled and done before the deadline. Right? Right.

- If you are in love with Tuck but are more in love with Columbia or Duke, feel free to apply to Tuck Early Action as long as you're ready and willing to pull your Tuck application with no remorse should one of those "binding" early-option schools admit you.

- If you really like Tuck but didn't get your act together (for the campus visit and interview!) in time for Early Action, then make it happen for the November Round.

- If you really truly honest totally like Tuck but maybe you only just heard about them or bschool or never thought about getting an MBA before and here it is December... well... you can absolutely apply in the January Round, but again, *make sure you get onto campus first if you can!* It's harder with the holidays, but at least there may be SNOW! So you'll have an authentic Tuck experience if you go.

Basically what we're saying is, apply as soon as you can, and if at all possible, do the on-campus interview thing first. If it's literally impossible for you to visit Hanover, then make every effort to apply in an earlier round, the earlier the better.

The 7 steps to a Tuck application

This is an ideal-world scenario but it's our strong recommendation – here is the ideal sequence of steps for putting together a Tuck application:

1. **Research the school** as much as you can – on the Internet, study the website, reach out to any alumni or student contacts you may have, all the other obvious first steps. Figure out what they're about and why you want to go there.

2. **Attend a Tuck info session in your area** if you can – these typically are scheduled starting in August and the schools are often on the road throughout the Fall. They have a schedule on their website. (Note: The Tuck Coffees, while valuable, are not the same; those are with Tuck alumni, and not typically with any admissions staff. The Tuck Receptions are the ones with admissions people and a formal presentation) Sign up for Tuck's email list and you'll hear about events as they're scheduled. Use the info session to figure out what they're about and why you want to go there.

3. **As soon as openings are available, schedule a campus visit and interview.** These fill up quickly! Monitor the website for news.

4. **Write at least a first draft of your career goals essay. This is a very important early step in the process.** Figure out what they're about and why you want to go there. You need to know this stuff in order to interview!

5. **Practice for your interview.** This involves rehearsing your answers to common questions about why you want an MBA, what are your career goals, why you want to go to Tuck, etc. **Everyone needs to practice;** do not just assume you can go into the interview cold and wow them. Look to the EssaySnark blahg for more interview tips and tricks, as well as the section at the end of this *Guide*. This is important. Be prepared to talk about what Tuck is about and why you want to go there.

6. **Go up to Hanover, tour the school, have your interview** – and have fun! And take notes. You'll learn a lot through this experience. Be sure to capture the names of people you speak with and jot down what you talked about – you can use this in your essays. Be prepared to talk about your career goals, and why you want to go to Tuck – and also absorb absorb absorb. Write down new insights about Tuck – and why you want to go there.

7. **Come home and finish your essays.** Do a second draft on your career goals essay, and dive into the other(s). You'll want to *demonstrate that you know what Tuck is about and why you want to go there.* (Are you getting that point yet?) Insert references to conversations you had while on campus and those insights that you gained from the experience.

Again, this is one school (the only school?) where EssaySnark really strongly without equivocation encourages you to go visit before applying. It won't kill your chances if you absolutely cannot do so, but yes it CAN make a difference. You should visit all the schools before you apply, but Tuck is the one that you *have* to visit.

"But EssaySnark," we hear you say, "I only just found out about this interview thing. I thought Tuck was like other schools where they only interview applicants by invitation, after I submit. Since I found out so late, when I went online to schedule my interview, they said that they don't have any more appointments available. EssaySnark, I know you said to do it, but it looks like I can't go up to campus because they don't have any slots left. Sorry, EssaySnark. I tried to follow your advice, but it looks like it's not going to happen."

You know what, Brave Supplicant? **EssaySnark still thinks you should go visit campus.** Even if they don't have any formal interview appointments available, *there is still value with you going to the school and seeing what they're about.* And, you never know — maybe someone will cancel and they'll be able to get you an interview appointment when you're there. *No matter what, it says good things about you as a candidate if you put forth the effort to do this.* This particular school encourages the visit — why not do everything in your power to do the things that they say are important??

Just a crazy thought, Brave Supplicant, but these are crazy times.

Multi-school strategies

Are you applying to multiple schools? You don't have to, but most people do. You could get your heart set on just one — like, say, *Tuck* — and go all-out to make it happen. EssaySnark *loves* those kinds of stories when that all pans out. Few people do that though.

So, since you're applying to multiple schools... and if you've got enough runway ahead of you to pull this off, in terms of timing of applications and deadlines — then here's another useful tip to consider:

Snarky Strategy #3

Do the Tuck essays first. They will be easier than many other schools' obtuse and convoluted essay questions.

Tuck's questions are so straightforward. And they're giving you so much room to answer them. Writing bschool essays is an acquired skill. Don't cut your teeth on harder essays than you need to. Skip Harvard and start with Tuck. It doesn't matter that the HBS deadline is sooner; you'll waste time needlessly if you don't optimize your workload and plan your strategy efficiently.

That's a pretty great segue, actually:

Planning Your Tuck Essays

Before we get too far with this, Tuck has very gentle language around the length limits on their essays. We need to nip this in the bud: They say 500 words. Make your essays 500 words. You can go over a little – but consider that they're giving you more room than practically any other school out there. Please don't go to 550 words on each of these three essays. A tiny bit over is fine; an excessive amount, no. You should be able to get your message across in 500-ish words just fine.

No, the schools do not count words. You do not have to be exact on any of your essays, for Tuck or for any school (except for ISB, which literally cuts you off if you go over). But, the adcoms have been reading essays for, like, awhile now. They can eyeball an essay and tell if it's heavy. Don't try anything cutsie like tiny fonts or infinitesimally narrow margins. Go with a standard professional document layout. You can't pull a fast one on these people, they've seen it all, it won't fly. Just get out the red pen and go to work. Yes it's painful to cut your precious words, but EssaySnark insists.

500 words.

Give or take.

Don't be abusive. Respect your reader's time. "Just the facts, ma'am." Tell the story and move on.

OK, let's talk about what goes in these puppies, then.

What's the right balance of topics?

The bulk of all your essays – in any application, to any bschool – should always be weighted towards heavyduty professional stories.

For Tuck, and the 2014 questions, ALL of your essays should be weighted this way.

Specifically:

- Essay 1: This should be completely professional (obviously)
- Essay 2: It's strongly recommended that this be a strictly professional story, though this is not required; a community engagement story *might* work

Are you ready to dive in?

Essay 1: Career Goals

If you've read any of the other *SnarkStrategies Guides* – particularly the one for Columbia – then you know how much emphasis to put on career goals in your MBA application. For almost every school, being exceptionally specific is the way to go. If you've done a good job with your career goals for Columbia, then you're going to be in fine shape for most any other school, particularly Tuck. (Sorry for the repeated references to Columbia, but it is a popular program that many of the Brave Supplicants we work with are interested in, and they've got a more stringent focus on career goals than any other school, so it's a useful reference for us.)

If you have not yet written a single word in any other career goals essay, then it's absolutely fine to tackle Tuck's version of same as your first foray into this wilderness.

And, if that's what you're now doing, here's the first step. This is what we recommend all our new clients go through to launch into this adventure: an exercise that we call developing your "Career Goal Statement."

EssaySnark's career goals exercise for new clients

Please complete this fill-in-the-blank exercise. This is a good first step for you to develop your ideas for career goals, in order to demonstrate to the adcom what you want to do and why an MBA is essential:

1. "After I get my MBA I will be/do X" [add as much detail as you can - job title, industry or niche, functional area, specialty, example companies to work for, geography, etc.].

[Write your answer here. Go ahead. Nobody will look at it.]

_____

_____

_____

_____

2. "My long term goal is to do Y" [less detail needed but must be clear and specific, and rational, given the s/t goal]

[Write this one down, too.]

_____

_____

_____

_____

> **3. "An MBA from Tuck is critical for me to achieve this because..."** [solid reasons that point to the differentiation offered by Tuck are critical here — you'll want to express how it will explicitly give you the skills you need for the short-term goal – it's fine if you don't have this nailed yet, you'll learn much more from your campus visit and other research]
>
> *[This bit is important. Use more space if you need to.]*
>
> _____
>
> _____
>
> _____
>
> **4. "Now is the right time for me to get an MBA because..."** [How will an MBA let you take advantage of the opportunities you see in your industry? If you're much younger than 28 – the average age of Tuck students – then it will be especially important for you to proactively address this]
>
> *["Why now" is implicitly embedded within Tuck's version of the career goals question.]*
>
> _____
>
> _____
>
> _____
>
> _____
>
> The short-term goal should have significant detail, and the bschool experience needs to be the setup for that (bschool should be positioned as the best means possible to prepare you for that s/t goal). The long-term goal needs much less detail but it needs to be logical and achievable, given the interim goals. You wouldn't want to position bschool as prep for the l/t goal, only the short-term one.

Yes, even though Tuck hasn't explicitly asked for a "job title" in their short-answer question, it wouldn't hurt to put one in. The specificity can take you far. It shows that you've put some thought into it, that you've researched the options, that you know the industry. That level of detail truly cannot hurt you.

You should spend some time on this. What most people come up with their first time out is far from sufficient. You may even need to go off and do some research on your target industry and find out what types of jobs are available and what you'd be doing in them. Do some digging. Flesh this out. An off-the-cuff set of career goals will not help you get into Tuck or any other top MBA program.

So what's a bad career goal?

Let's look at a few examples, so that you can see what not to do.

> "I want to become a leader in the financial services industry."

We see this all the time. Sorry folks. "Leader" is meaningless. And, believe it or not, so is "financial services." Much too broad. Are you talking about a big bank? A hedge fund? A mutual fund or other investment management company? Even insurance companies are often lumped into "financial services." This sentence is near-meaningless. It doesn't tell us anything about *what you want to do*.

Here's another one:

> "I want to be on the executive team of a multinational corporation."

Same problem. Sure, "executive team" has a little more specificity than "leader" however it still doesn't tell us *what you want to do*. (Note the theme?) And "multinational corporation" is just a blob of a term. What type of corporation? In which country? If you're interested in some type of international angle to your career, then you need to say that! This term is communicating next to nothing — except to say that maybe you haven't put that much thought into it yet.

The other issue with both of these "bad" examples (probably) is timing.

It's unrealistic to assume you'll be much of a "leader" — at least, not on a grand scale or anything — within the timeframe that Tuck is expecting you to present with these goals. Nobody can see the future. Nobody knows what you'll be doing in 15 years. And yet that's how long it would take – *minimum* – for most people to gain the experience, skills, and connections to actually become a CEO or what have you. It's highly unlikely you'll be rocking that particular boat within the timeframe expected in a "short/long-term goals" question from any school. So, saying you'll be on the ELT of a big conglomerate is a little unrealistic, probably.

Instead, you need to focus on literally what type of job you'll get right when you come out of Tuck, and then, carve out a plan for how you'll progress from there, to perhaps another position, and at most, one more, which you'll identify as your long-term target. That final job that you present as your long-term goal should be within a reasonable timeframe. The foreseeable future. Like, maybe ten years from now, max (even that is not really "foreseeable" given how quickly things change in our lives and the world these days).

Keep in mind that most people are promoted maybe once every two years. If you consider your long-term goal to be in the five- to eight-year post-MBA timeframe, that will help you see (hopefully) what might be a realistic target to present for the adcom. **Given where you're at today in your career (level/role/title/responsibilities), what is a probable trajectory for you to end up in, say, the year 2022?**

If you need a little more space to capture your thinking on your long-term goal, go right ahead:

One exception where it might fly to tell the adcom that you'll be "CEO"? If you're going to be working in a family business after you graduate. If that's the case, then it's fine to say you're going to be taking over the whole show. You have different challenges than most people in presenting your goals (which are outside the discussion of this *Guide*) however this could work well in being realistic and believable.

What did we just say? Something about "realistic and believable"? Yes, that sounds good. This is something to make note of formally and officially. In fact, let's call it:

Snarky Strategy #4

Your career goals must be *believable* and *achievable*.

We've alluded to this already, with the comments about timeframe and what's feasible to accomplish in the long-term goal horizon that the school expects. The Tuck adcom is going to look at your goals and see if they make sense. Is this a plan that you will be able to pull off? Is it do-able? Or more like a pipe dream?

An important point to make at this juncture is: *Don't make stuff up*. The point of this exercise is not to present the most amazing, aggressive, flamboyant-sounding goals the school has ever seen. Actually, it's usually much more effective to present goals that are very standard, traditional, perhaps even run-of-the-mill.

Bschool candidates are always told that they have to stand out, that they have to differentiate themselves. Well guess what? The career goals essay is not the place to do this.

- **People are admitted to Tuck because they have clear, rational, logical goals that gives the adcom a feeling of confidence – where it's clear that the candidate will be successful with her plan.**

- **People are admitted to Tuck because – as EssaySnark has already laid out for you – they show *enthusiasm*, *commitment*, and an *appreciation for what Tuck is about* – plus, they demonstrate that they have a real "need" for the MBA. All this has to come through in other essays too (particularly essay 4).**

The best way to impress the Tuck adcom is to show them that you've already built your career up to a certain point – this is the "quality" of work experience that they look for – and that you have a plan for where you want to take it from here, and you're looking for the advantage of a Tuck MBA to do so. This means, you want to present career goals that MAKE SENSE, both given who YOU are, and given what Tuck stands for and what they can offer to you.

If you've read the *SnarkStrategies Guide* for either Columbia or Berkeley-Haas or UCLA or Kellogg, then you will recognize that this is similar advice to what EssaySnark provided there. But the key difference is that *all these schools are quite different*. You might be able to use the same standard career goals for these particular schools – and in fact, you should, because you're the same person applying to all of them, so why the heck would your goals change simply because it's a different application? But you'll need to express your understanding of and appreciation for the respective schools' culture quite differently if you want to be successful at each. It's rather unusual that someone gets an offer from both Columbia and Tuck unless they do their homework on each school individually and understand what they're about, and demonstrate that understanding within their presentation.

Perhaps more than most, Tuck cares about "school fit" an awful lot. "School fit" is an expression of the school's culture, and how you resonate with those qualities. It's a little subtle and perhaps somewhat esoteric, but it's very obvious when it's expressed appropriately in an application (and when it's not!). Again, you have your work cut out for you in how you address the quintessential "school fit" question that is Tuck Essay 4. However all your essays for Tuck need to work together in tandem to express to the adcom that you're the type of person who will fit in well with who they are and what they're about.

A few additional warnings:

- If you're looking to use bschool to make some **radical career change**, you have a bigger challenge. You need to show the adcom that you have transferable skills and are equipped to make the transition to the new field. This can be especially critical for those going in a dissimilar direction, e.g., IT guys wanting to go into finance. You'll need to show how you're ready to make this leap.

- Conversely, if you're not showing ENOUGH transition — if your stated **short-term goal is too similar** (or even identical) to what you are already currently doing in your job today — then you're not giving the adcom enough evidence of why you need an MBA. You should position yourself as ADVANCING, and then show how the MBA is the one main requirement that you need to get from A to B.

A Snarky Caveat

The three most common mistakes with bschool career goals are:

- **They're too vague**

- **They're too ambitious**

- **They're too broad**

If your goals suffer from any of these sins, it's highly unlikely that Tuck will let you in.

- ***Too vague*** means saying you want to work in "financial services" or on an "executive team" or that you want to go into "international business." None of these are careers, they are concepts.

- ***Too ambitious*** is a goal that's written to impress the reader instead of being attainable for the candidate's actual skills and experience – often goals that involve starting a company/nonprofit/private equity fund fall into this category. It's fine to have an entrepreneurial goal, provided you lay the foundation appropriately for it.

- ***Too broad*** frequently happens when the applicant can't make up his mind and so he brings in multiple options of "I could do this or I might do that." While it could very well be true that you will pursue different options and paths once you're in the process of earning your MBA, it is usually a mistake to try and present all these different options to the adcom in their essays. There simply isn't room to provide an appropriate level of detail on more than one possible career path.

The Tuck adcom tends to reward candidates who express confidence and conviction, who sound like they have an honest-to-goodness action plan. Sure, your life may take you in a different direction once the wheels are in motion. What the bschool folks want to see is that you're mature and responsible, that you know how to take control of your life and that you're able to make your own success. A well-crafted set of essays will communicate this implicitly. Keeping that *realistic and believable* guideline in mind as you refine your goals should help you avoid these problems.

OK, are you confident about your career goals? Good, because we're moving on to the actual essay now.

What needs to go in Tuck's career goals essay?

Here's the question:

> Why is an MBA a critical next step toward your short- and long-term career goals? Why is Tuck the best MBA fit for you and your goals and why are you the best fit for Tuck?

First, this essay needs to FOCUS ON THE FUTURE. You'll notice they ask nothing about the past here. They can read your resume, and essay 2, and your recommendations, if they need to know your professional history.

That being said, it's definitely relevant, and highly recommended, to include a quick recap of who you are/what you've done, to set context, but do not go overboard. There should be no more than a couple sentences of background info.

A straightforward structure for Tuck 1 is — and this is just an example, your essay need not conform to this exactly:

- **INTRO:** EssaySnark always likes to see the actual career goals stated in the opening, either in the very first sentence, or at least somewhere in the intro paragraph. Because of how Tuck has phrased their version of the career goals question, we feel it's actually VERY important to literally answer that upfront. Right. Here. Now. Bam! You could potentially include a quick bit of background info in this paragraph, too, with a summary of what you've done and how it's made you ready for this next step. The "readiness" should be expressed somewhere; it can go here or elsewhere, it's up to you.

- **PARA 2: Short-term goal. Next** you should flesh out what you stated in that first paragraph. Define/explain/express/illustrate what you want to do when you graduate from Tuck. This is THE MOST IMPORTANT part of the essay — perhaps of the entire application. You want *details* here. If you didn't include some background info in the intro, then you should do something with that here (something like, "I am ready for this next challenge because..." or "My X years in consulting gave me the such-and-such skills that I need to do this" or whatever).

- **PARA 3: Long-term goal.** This paragraph can be much shorter than the previous one, and some people are even able to include the long-term goal within the discussion of short-term goal, but it's important to have a distinct set of two separate goals, and it's usually helpful to the adcom if you have a separate discussion of each. You need much less detail here; it does not need to be as long as the previous paragraph, but the reader should be able to easily identify the short-term and the long-term goal as discrete items in the essay.

- **PARA 4:** Why MBA/why Tuck? The focus should be on the latter question, which implicitly answers the former. Why have you chosen Tuck, over the gazillion other great schools out there, to achieve these stated goals? And just as important: Why do you fit their culture? This is where you seed in specifics like classes, faculty, clubs, programs, resources, etc. Tell them that you visited campus on [date] and got all inspired by [such and such]. Show them how much homework you've done. But, make it relevant. Link in these school-specific references to your exact needs — talk about why each matters *to you*. Do a gap analysis — see where you're lacking and how the graduate education from Dartmouth can fill those gaps, then identify the resources that will do it. This can be hard skills, soft skills, or both. Make all this tailored to Tuck. And PLEASE do not let EssaySnark catch you breathing even one whiff of a sentence like "Tuck is a top-ranked program" – it is COMPLETELY IRRELEVANT to your pitch to bschool that Tuck made it to the #1 spot on anyone's list.

Also, keep in mind that you're getting the opportunity to cover Tuck-specific material in each of the other essays. Be sure these pieces work well together.

- **CONCLUSION**: Wrap up with a recap of why you want an MBA from Tuck, ideally restating your career goals and/or referencing something specific about the program, and/or you personally, etc. Can be just a sentence or two.

Your career goals form the foundation of your application. This is a critical essay to get right at any school that asks about goals, but especially at Tuck.

Essay 2: Leadership

You may have noticed that EssaySnark hasn't really been harping on that perennial bschool theme of *leadership* in this *Guide*. It's not that leadership is unimportant at Tuck. Clearly that's not the case, given that they have just one more essay and that's all it's asking about. But *culture* and *commitment* and all those other things do trump leadership and teamwork, at least a bit – or maybe a better way to say it is that culture at Tuck encompasses all these other themes of leadership and teamwork, and even eclipses them individually.

But leadership is pretty darn important. Here's the proof, in Tuck essay 2:

> **Tell us about your most meaningful ~~collaborative~~ leadership experience and what role you played. What did you learn about your own individual strengths and weaknesses through this experience?**

Oh wait, there's a question in the back. Yes?

"What's with that deleted word there, EssaySnark? That 'collaborative' thing?"

Ahh. Good question, Brave Supplicant.

That's what Tuck asked with this question in 2013.

The 2012 essays featured a version of this question without the "collaborative" angle.

"Collaborative" Leadership?

While teamwork is of course important at Tuck, the fact that they ditched that word "collaborative" from the question yet kept the rest of it intact means that they care about LEADERSHIP.

If you're able to talk about *collaborative leadership* with a powerful story of how you had an impact in the context of working with others, then fine, use that. But only use it if it's your best story of *leadership* – don't use it just because it has an element of collaboration in it.

Anyway, we believe on close inspection that the word "collaborative" is redundant. Isn't all effective leadership about collaboration anyway? All leadership is about other people; we've never seen an example of a strong leadership story with one person operating in a vacuum. So working within a team is required. That's sort of in the main definition of "leadership"; there has to be others involved. And how can you lead others if you don't get their buy-in?

The fact that Tuck deleted that adjective does not mean that it's an unimportant concept. However, we assume that including it in last year's question distracted applicants from what Tuck really cares about, and that many people strained to find the right story that met both elements exactly. We saw people we worked with have trouble with incorporating both elements, and sometimes it led to some slightly less ideal essay topics.

Our takeaway message?

Don't sacrifice a story about how you have had influence and meaning in your work just because it doesn't specifically speak to "collaboration" as its foremost quality.

Or in other words:

Find your *most significant experience leading others* and talk about that. If you use the word "collaboration" in the essay, fine – but it's totally not necessary to do so.

How to choose a story for Tuck essay 2

We'll say that again:

Find your *most significant experience leading others* and talk about that.

Or in other words:

Focus on impact.

Impact is where the rubber meets the road with this essay.

Here's an exercise for you to start to identify some ideas for this essay. What does "leadership" mean to you? (If you're applying to Harvard, then this exercise will be uber important for that essay, too.)

Everyone knows what leadership is, right? But can you demonstrate it? This tends to be much more difficult a task than most people expect. Leadership is perhaps like beauty (in the eye of the beholder) but in the context of bschool essays, your job is to *convey* leadership to your reader. So what this means is you need to a) understand the qualities and attributes that make a good leader, and b) select a story from your background that can literally demonstrate or showcase those qualities in you.

This is not a trivial task.

Let's start at the beginning.

This exercise will help you begin to get your arms around leadership as a concept, so that you can have a better chance of articulating what it is and what it means to you, through a story that you will tell for the adcom. You need to make your understanding of leadership explicit, before you can write about it with any authority. This will be of great benefit when you begin to identify the stories that you might use in your essays and interview. Take this opportunity to brainstorm around the idea of "leadership."

First, define the word "leader" – don't just say what a leader does, but see if you can write out an actual dictionary-style definition (without looking at the dictionary, obviously):

_____

_____

In this essay, your task will be to highlight a specific example that shows what you have done in terms of leadership.

Look at the definition you just wrote. Go peek at the dictionary definition now if you need to.

Now, jot down the best examples that you can think of for when you've exhibited those "leaderly" traits – these can be from any context of your life, work, school, sports, community service, whatever:

_____

_____

It's OK if you don't come up with winning examples right away. This often requires some thought, and some effort, and some time and space – let this process breathe. Over the next few days, come back to these exercises again. Spend more time brainstorming on what leadership means, and also what collaboration is, and how you've been both so far in your life. Then identify actual incidents – projects, deals, wins, homeruns – events in your life where you knocked it out of the park. These should be big achievements that clearly highlight your leadership abilities.

When you start to narrow down the list and figure out which example might be the best to use for this essay, you should look at these criteria:

1. Which is *the most significant?* Significance can be defined in any number of ways, but it must be clear when you write the essay why you've used this story.
2. Which stories are *current?* The Tuck adcom doesn't have an explicit timeframe for you to stick within but the best stories are typically from the last three to five years.
3. Which stories are *from your professional experience?* This isn't mandatory but we strongly encourage you to use a professional story if you can.

Very important: YOU MUST BE EXPLICIT WHEN YOU TELL THIS STORY. You obviously do not have much room in the essay, though it's certainly longer than other schools allow for a similar question. The most important tactic in developing your material is that you very concisely must convey what you literally did that proves you're a leader.

Your *actions* are what will demonstrate to the reader that you had an impact.

You need to show a cause-and-effect relationship between what you actually did, and the outcomes you're citing. That's the "what role you played" part. You could also be very explicit and literally state what your role was in the engagement – were you the analyst, a marketing assistant, the swim coach? Be clear on who you were and who else was involved in the situation. Then talk about literally what you did to effect change among the group.

The biggest mistake that we see with these types of essays is that they are vague and operate at a very high level. You must give the reader a picture of who you are, based on the results that you brought to others – the customer, your team, your boss, your company, the charity that you were volunteering for. Quantified results are always ideal, though not a mandatory component of the story.

Of course, leadership is a concept that has a wide spectrum of definitions – this is where you can get creative in how you interpret the question and apply it to your life. Every single applicant will have a different story to tell that highlights different aspects of leadership (you can also highlight multiple aspects of leadership in a single story, you know).

Also, please remember that you need not have had a formal title that says "leader" in order to demonstrate that you've been one. Often the most compelling story is about a time when the applicant had to influence others from a lower-ranking role or without any official authority.

Assuming Kellogg maintains a similar approach for their 2014 essays (which have not yet been released as of the time of this writing), then if you're applying to Kellogg, you'll have a rare opportunity of synergy. In past years, Kellogg has asked for *multiple* examples of leadership (if they keep that question in 2014, then usually two examples is a good number in that essay). Here Tuck only wants the single "most meaningful" one.

Remember also: It's up to you to ascribe "meaning" to the story! If it's not obvious why you're selecting the story you have, you'd better interpret it for the reader by explaining why it was so important for you (or, that might be a hint that you're not choosing the strongest story you could). If you're applying to one of these other schools (e.g., in the past UC-Berkeley; TBD if they do it for 2014) that asks about "significant accomplishments", then one of the stories you've got in one of those essays might work here – or they might not. A "significant accomplishment" might involve leadership but it might not, though conversely, your "most meaningful leadership experience" almost definitely is going to also be a "significant accomplishment."

Please keep in mind that leadership typically involves other people. Hopefully this surfaced for you as part of your brainstorming exercises on leadership. That whole "collaborative" bit. Because EssaySnark doesn't want to be insulting or anything, but what is "leadership" if it is not about "leading"? And what are you "leading" if not other people?

By contrast, an "accomplishment" story for one of those other schools might be something that you achieved fully on your own, such as a personal tale about losing a significant amount of weight, or completing a marathon, etc. (though also note that a marathon story would be a little passé as a "significant accomplishment" story for a school the likes of Harvard; running a marathon is not quite in the "significant" category strongly enough to really qualify for that caliber of school).

OK, so that was just the first component to Tuck Essay 2.

What did you learn?

The second part of this essay gives you a chance to do a self-assessment. This is important; many people flub this part. You want to now show some insights and maturity in how you discuss the situation – not only in patting yourself on the back with a couple "atta boys" about how great you pulled it off, but ALSO – very important!! – in identifying a thing or two that you could've done better. You want to talk about where your developmental areas are, and you want to do THAT in the context of what you're hoping to gain from the MBA. Oh wait – not just what you want to get out of the MBA, but *what you want to get out of the MBA from Tuck*. Yeah. All that.

The best essay 2s present a REALLY BIG STORY of something impactful that you pulled off, as the first half of the essay. Then, they talk about the reasons why you were successful – and these should hopefully be strengths and qualities that will set you up for success in whatever you've stated as your career goals in Essay 1. AND – yes there's more – you need to talk about what you could've done better, and what this taught you about yourself, in the context of what else you need in your ongoing growth as a current and future leader. *AND* ideally you will link THAT to what Tuck can give you.

Whew!

Additional guidelines for what's an ideal story for Essay 2:

- Typically a professional story is best, though this is not mandatory.
- The story must demonstrate obvious qualities and strengths – the reader must be able to see the coolness that you have within you, that you used to great effect to pull this off
- It should be focused on *leading people*
- Ideally it will be from the past three years; under no circumstances should you go back to college or earlier for this story.

EssaySnark feels pretty strongly about that last point. Even though we gave you free reign to include any such ideas in your brainstorming exercise from earlier, that was just a technique to allow you freedom of thought. This essay positively should be a recent one. If you haven't got any evidence of being a leader in the past few years, then why on earth are you looking at business school?

So many Brave Supplicants come to us proposing some story that they have from their past, maybe it's the lacrosse team in college, or some sorority story, or how they won the spelling bee in fifth grade – and they want our blessing to use this story, even though they heard us state very directly our "focus on the past three years" guideline.

Why do we say "within the past three years"? A bunch of reasons:

1. That's what Stanford and MIT have defined for their essays for many years; even though Stanford has lifted this restriction in 2014 it is still relevant. No, Tuck is not Stanford, though we like them both as much. But if Stanford feels that recent experiences are more relevant for their purposes in evaluating your candidacy... don't you think that any adcom would feel the same? Trust us, they do.

2. Giving the adcom the goods from your recent past is the best way to convince them that you're at the right point in your career to benefit from the super-special opportunity that is a Tuck MBA. You need to be pulling out all the stops to wow them with your readiness. Stories that happened not too long ago are much more informative about who you actually are TODAY than ones from ancient history.

3. Tuck prefers older candidates, who've been in the workforce and have done impressive things in their careers. The average age is 28. If you want to go back to *college days* for a story to present to Tuck... well, isn't that perhaps highlighting the wrong part of your life?

4. If all ya got is a story from 10 years ago... basically you're saying to the adcom, "Sorry, that's the best I got, I haven't done smack with my life since then." You do not want to seem like a one-hit wonder. If all you have to offer are stories from long ago, sorry my dear, you're just not going to come off as all that impressive of a candidate to the reader.

So within the past three years or so is great – just don't make it *too* recent. Because if you talk about something that happened, like, last week, how the heck could you know that it was already the "most meaningful" in your life? Usually events in our lives need time to ripen or percolate or whatever before we understand their significance. Plus, if it just happened – particularly if it's a volunteer work story – well, that just smells too much of *candidate-went-out-and-created-a-story-for-purposes-of-MBA-applications*. So, not too recent, and not too old.

Now, you may have noticed that this essay question does not ask anything about Tuck per se – but *all* your essays should be tailored to Tuck. Here is another chance for you to incorporate your 'why I love Tuck' material – maybe you couldn't fit it all into essay 1 (you probably could not -- if you've done your homework appropriately you'll have way more reasons for why you want to go to Tuck than you can fit in a short single essay). So here's more room for you to include those reasons.

Another big angle on this essay that the adcom will be watching for – and this is key – are you listening?? *This essay question lets you show your maturity, demonstrate your self-awareness, and certainly present your humility.* There's a way to talk about leadership experiences in a positive, impactful way – but sometimes people end up doing so in a way that makes them look like real jerks. We already covered that; don't be that guy (or chick). Focus on how you achieved the results that you're claiming, based on the actual and direct actions that you took to bring change to the situation, and do so in a way that showcases your personality and soft skills along with the achievement itself.

That, my friend, will make for a winner.

The best story for Tuck Essay 2 will take advantage of

Snarky Strategy #5

Use this story to show how you are ready to pursue the goals you stated in Essay 1.

For example, if Essay 1 talks about your entrepreneurial goals, then perhaps Essay 2 can demonstrate that you have an entrepreneurial mindset – even if you've not formally started a company before. Or, that you take calculated risks. You are painting a picture of who you are and what your skills are based on the story you tell in essay 2, and the best story for essay 2 is one that reinforces the things you'll need in order to pursue the goals that you're pitching them.

Do some reflection on what you need in order to be successful in this new career you're laying out (remember the exercise from page 22?) Give the adcom a story in essay 2 *that presents these qualities.*

That will be the smartest way to go with these two short essays, Brave Supplicant.

Letters of Recommendation

A tiny change that Tuck implemented for 2014 is that they changed the name of what they call recommendations.

They used to call them "Confidential Statements of Qualifications."

Now they call them what everyone else calls them: "Letters of Recommendation."

Despite this welcome effort to standardize, you shouldn't lose sight of that original name.

The job of your recommenders is to show how you are *qualified*.

With the smaller application and fewer essays this year, it's even more important for recommenders to do that.

Remember that list of leadership examples that you came up with in the Essay 2 planning section (page 31)? Well, you can only use one in Tuck Essay 2 – but you can totally use the others for your recommendations.

Or more accurately: *You can suggest that your recommenders use the others in what they write about you.*

You cannot write your own recommendations. But you can work with your recommenders so that they have some good stories to use on your behalf.

We have an App Accelerator on Letters of Recommendation in case you're stuck on who you should be choosing for this very important deliverable, and we also have Recommender's Instruction Sets available to help guide your recommenders on how to tackle the different requirements from the specific schools that you're targeting. Both of these can be found on essaysnark.com.

Another great resource to help your recommenders: This video from Admissions Director Dawna Clark:

http://youtu.be/DC_rPHlaPPw

Lastly, the other key points to be aware of with Tuck's recommendations: In 2013, they added some new questions that recommenders are asked, about MATURITY and about QUANT SKILLS. This also gives a very strong indication of the traits that they care about. You need to be expressing these sufficiently across your app – in the recommendations and everywhere else – in order to be seen as a qualified candidate to this school. Feel free to discuss these points with your recommenders when you bring them on board to help you.

International Experience

At the beginning of this guide, we mentioned how much Tuck values international experience. If you haven't dug into their online application, then you may not have noticed that they actually ask you a specific question about this. (We're assuming that they will keep this question with 2014; as of this writing, the app hadn't been released yet for us to check.)

If you want to know how important this is and how to handle it, we refer you directly to the source – a video answer from Tuck Admissions Director Dawna Clark:

http://youtu.be/YboFYnrJN1g

If you're not reading this on the internet then basically what she says is:

1. Recruiters are asking for Tuck grads to have more international experience.

2. International experience is not a requirement for admission (though we do see it correlated with admissions success). Because of the global environment that we all work in now, as part of the admissions process, Tuck is now asking you to describe what your international experience has been, so that they can understand your profile better.

3. Good examples to mention in answering this question in the application are exactly as you would expect: a study abroad experience during college, an overseas work assignment, or personal travel.

This answer does not need to be involved. We have a tip for you though: If you talk about some international work experience in this mini-essay, then you also should have them on your resume! It should be very easy for someone skimming the resume to pick out those experiences (this is a smart strategy to use when applying to any school; few other American schools have separate questions on international experience like Tuck does, so you want your resume to highlight those experiences for your adcoms). Make sure that all aspects of your application support and reinforce the others. No gaps. If you have some important overseas trip that you did through work that you use for this answer, find a way to also reference it (by city/country) on the resume, too.

Also, when you present your information on what you've done and where, in terms of these international experiences, be sure to say WHEN and HOW LONG you were in the foreign country.

A final bit of advice: Even though Ms. Clark says in that video that if you haven't had much experience overseas, you can get some at Tuck, we do NOT recommend that you use that for your answer. Try to find some other example of your cross-cultural fluency to present in this essay. She has a good example of what one person did before, which you can use for ideas.

You CAN talk about your interest in those overseas trips while your at Tuck as part of Essay 1, which is typically the better place for such statements.

Optional Essay

This advice is true for any school, not just Tuck: If you don't have something specific that is a) important; and b) that you just cannot for the life of you figure out how to cover appropriately in the main essays... then you should write the optional essay.

BUT: Tuck gives you an awful lot of essay real estate to cover an awful lot of territory. Are you sure you cannot fit your other-thing into one of those spaces?

For example, if you had poor grades in college because your mother got sick... that sounds like an ideal topic for Tuck Essay 4.

If you have a gap in your resume because you were unemployed for six months after the economy fell apart in 2008... could be a prime candidate for Essay 3 (maybe; we've actually seen fairly lame renditions of this particular subject matter in this particular essay, so make sure it's really showcasing something positive about you – please, no whining in bschool essays!!). Or, an astute and creative applicant might find a way to explain a gap in employment in Essay 1.

For any school, Tuck included, your strategy should be to not overstay your welcome. Like a polite and respectful guest, you should enter the Tuck admissions team's domain, offering exactly what they have asked for in their essay prompts and application instructions, and then exit gracefully.

A relevant subject to cover in the optional essay is a low GPA, provided that you actually have real information to provide to help the adcom understand what was going on with you during your undergraduate experience. Appropriate essays on grades might cover items such as working your way through college, or an extreme personal situation like the illness of a family member. That sort of thing. You probably will not gain points for honesty by just saying that you were didn't take school seriously and were partying too much. We cover the perennial question of "what to do about a low GPA" on our blahg:

http://essaysnark.com/2010/05/omg-2-posts-in-2-days.html

The one item that is pretty much mandatory to cover in an optional essay for Tuck is if you are not getting a letter of recommendation from your current direct supervisor. If you don't want to alert your boss that you might be leaving soon to go back to school, that's perfectly fine and legit. You should simply explain the situation (briefly!) in the optional essay, and tell the adcom why you chose the recommenders that you did instead of your supervisor. Ideally in such a case, at least one of your recommenders will be a supervisor from a previous job.

Keep in mind that this optional essay should be SHORT. If all you're doing is explaining your choice of recommenders, there's no reason why it should go on past a paragraph. If you have multiple issues to explain, you can include them all in a single optional essay. Your final length for this one should not go past 500 words, and much, much shorter is infinitely better.

Remember: Do not outstay your welcome! You may think that writing essays is hard, but EssaySnark can tell you, reading them for days on end is absolutely exhausting. Do not submit more to the adcom than they truly need in order to understand who you are and what you're about.

There's also a **reapplicant essay**, however if that's you, then we strongly encourage you to pick up the *Reapplicant's Guide*, since there's way more to developing that strategy than we can hope to cover in just a few short pages here. Tuck is fond of reapplicants so you do have a shot at it, but you also need to make sure that you fix the errors committed in the last app and show them why now you're really ready.

Finally: Don't forget there's also a separate essay for the Tuck scholarship application. We have a targeted QuickSnark Guide on the Tuck Scholarship available for instant-access purchase on essaysnark.com, if you want some help with that.

The Tuck Interview

So we got you all worked up in the beginning of this guide about how you HAVE to go on campus and interview... did you really think we were going to wrap up this *SnarkStrategies Guide* without giving you more specific guidance on how to go about preparing for that?

These tips are important for an interview at any school, yet they're geared towards the interview experience at Tuck. Here are some facts of how things are done in Dartmouth:

- You will likely be interviewed by a specially-trained and super-nice second-year student if you go on campus for your applicant-initiated interview. If you skip that step and apply without an interview, and are then invited to do one, then it will be more likely conducted by a member of the admissions committee (though it's still possible that you'll end up with a student interviewer if you go to campus). Skype interviews for people who can't make it in person are typically done by admissions staff. All interviews are treated equally, regardless of who conducts them and how. Significantly: Alumni rarely do interviews at Tuck these days.

- You cannot know in advance what they will ask you. Part of your preparation should be in getting comfortable responding to any random question about yourself.

- Your preparation should consist of a) having your career goals already mapped out; see page 17; b) practicing your answers to common questions like *Why do you want an MBA?* by speaking them out loud – don't just say the answers in your head; and c) practicing some more with a friend who goes through the questions with you. You can find bschool interview questions all over the Internet, EssaySnark isn't going to clutter up this Guide with a list of them. The point is, *practice*.

- It's likely that most of the questions will focus on the same types of things they ask in the essays: what are your career goals, tell me about leadership, why do you want to go to Tuck.

- Bring two copies of your resume, one for your interviewer, and one for you. That way, you have it in front of yourself to reference as you talk. It's much easier to follow along with what you're saying about yourself if you have the same piece of paper in front of you as the interviewer does.

- The answers that you give in the interview must sync up with what you end up saying in the essays that you submit. If you change your career goals, for example, between the time of your interview and the time that you submit your application, well, you'd better explain what's up with that somewhere! Don't assume they won't notice.

- Dress professionally, yes, in a suit. Yes, you'll likely be more formally dressed than your interviewer; what's the problem with that? You're the one trying to get in, they already are in. If you want more guidance on how to prepare for a school visit, check out the EssaySnark blahg for some tips.

- Be exceptionally polite. Arrive early, but not too early. Say please and thank you.

- Send a follow-up note afterwards. Everything counts.

What to Do Next

This is not meant as your complete guide to Tuck. It is meant to point you in the right direction on the *Tuck essays* – but you already know what we're going to say next:

You really got to get to Hanover. Tour the campus. See the mountains. Sit in on a class. Ask questions. Meet the Tuckies.

Then you'll know where to go next.

One final request – we rarely ask for much from you Brave Supplicants so we're hoping you might consider doing this:

On the Tuck application, it asks "Where did you learn about Tuck?" This is an optional question. You can leave it blank.

However, if you happened to have been introduced to Tuck through EssaySnark – say, by us suggesting you consider them when we did your Comprehensive Profile Review, or by reading about it on the blahg – well, it would be kinda awesome if you would put our name down there. As you saw from the Tuck adcom tweet we quoted on the opening pages of this guide, Tuck Admissions knows all about us – and Tuck is very open to applicants using admissions consultant. See this video from the admissions director as proof: http://youtu.be/n0frzLgUL8w – thanks, Sandeep, for asking that question! We pride ourselves on providing ethical consulting and we also appreciate strong relationships with the admissions team, so we would be so grateful if you were to do that.

And finally: If for some reason you don't make it in to Tuck this year, remember that they're friendly to reapplicants, and they often will offer feedback to denied candidates in the Spring. If you end up in that position, then call them up and ask about it. They're one of the friendliest admissions teams out there. They want you to succeed.

And so do we!

EssaySnark reviews essays for the top business schools on our blahg (for free!) at http://essaysnark.com. If you're an especially brave Brave Supplicant, you can send over a draft or three and we may post a full critique of one on the site. And, if you have questions we can help with about Tuck or any of your other target schools, don't hesitate to email us at gethelpnow@essaysnark.com or find us on Twitter (@EssaySnark).

Look for other *SnarkStrategies Guides* (digital and paperback) at your favorite bookseller or on the EssaySnark blahg.

FOLLOW ESSAYSNARK ON TWITTER!

"Like all magnificent things, it's very simple."

TUCK EVERLASTING

www.ingramcontent.com/pod-product-compliance
Lightning Source LLC
Chambersburg PA
CBHW080527110426
42742CB00017B/3265